A Bear-y Merry Christmas

RAHSAAN ARMAND/ANITA ARMAND

Balboa Press books may be ordered through booksellers or by contacting:

Balboa Press
A Division of Hay House
1663 Liberty Drive
Bloomington, IN 47403
www.balboapress.com
844-682-1282

Because of the dynamic nature of the Internet, any web addresses or links contained in this book may have changed since publication and may no longer be valid. The views expressed in this work are solely those of the author and do not necessarily reflect the views of the publisher, and the publisher hereby disclaims any responsibility for them.

Any people depicted in stock imagery provided by Getty Images are models, and such images are being used for illustrative purposes only.
Certain stock imagery © Getty Images.

ISBN: 978-1-9822-5890-0 (sc)
ISBN: 978-1-9822-5891-7 (e)

Library of Congress Control Number: 2020922611

Print information available on the last page.

Balboa Press rev. date: 12/03/2020

*C*hristmas is a GREAT time for everyone. It's filled with happiness, family, friends, and FUN!

"A Bear-y Merry Christmas" is the highlight of the year — laughs, good times and plenty of joy and cheer. It is the best wit' "Poppa Bear," "Momma Bear," "Claire-A-Bear," all three. Oh, there's also "Tootie Bear," "Gummie Bear" and "Cub-y Bear — that's me.

This is our story of a Bear-y Merry Christmas...

Two days before Christmas, time was ticking faster.
Poppa Bear was working — he is a pastor.

Poppa Bear preaches and teaches from the Bible.
He hopes his message will one day go viral:
"Jesus is the reason for the season."

'The day before a Bear-y Merry
Christmas, the "gurls" hit
the mall; the Christmas tree
was standing, nice and tall.

We are shopping for last minute
gifts: for cousins, nieces, nephews,
aunts, uncles, and friends...
"...Oh my," I thought, "How
much will we have to spend?"

'Twas the night before Christmas, our house was set.

Claire-A-Bear adds decorations to the tree. They look good to me.

I guess I'll add my touch to the tree; after all, Santa is coming to bless us — all three.

Momma Bear hurries to get her "hair did."

I'm glad, because her head was looking like a squid! 😜

<Just kidding>

Momma Bear is always fair, even when she doesn't do her hair.

Tootie Bear got her "wig did" too. Methinks she's
ready for a Bear-y Merry Christmas with you.

Momma Bear hangs our stockings with care,
knowing *Saint Nicholas* soon will be there.

We call Gummie Bear to check on Christmas in the Midwest. Having a BIG sister really is the BEST.

Claire-A-Bear thought she'd
hide to catch a glimpse of Santa.
Don't she know, he'll throw
sand in her eyes and we'll be
yelling, "What's the matter!?"

Maybe I should tell her
to get to bed, so "Bear-y
Merry Christmas" can
hurry and be said!

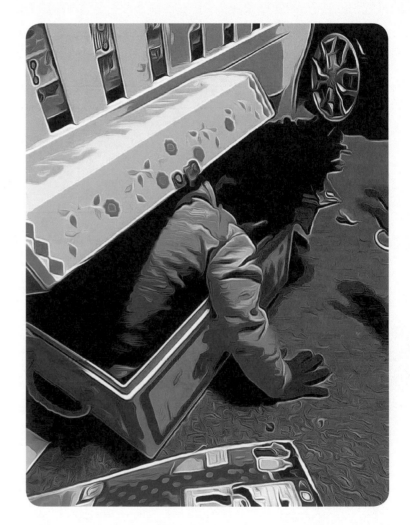

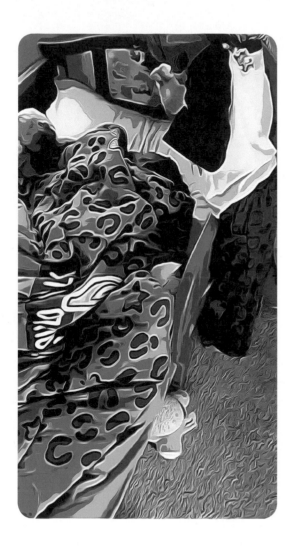

It is Christmas Day!
Claire-A-Bear shakes me and she wakes me.

"Get up. Get up," she shouts. "It's time for
the Bear-y Merry Christmas," sissy touts.

We hurry downstairs in hopes that Jesus has answered our prayers!

He did. He did. God sent Santa!

But he forgot his

cookies and his milk.

They could've been helpful on his way to Atlanta! ☹

I'm Bear-y happy — a bike,
dolls, and even a play oven!

All this stuff, I'm really luvin'!

What's that Claire-A-Bear smells?

"A camper car, a camper
car," she yells.

Claire-A-Bear says,

"Boy oh boy!
Geesh, there are just so many toys."

Poppa Bear has a great idea.
"Since God has been good
to y'all this year, pack up
your old toys and give them
away with great cheer!"

"These will be great," Claire-A-Bear thinks; she
looks at me, I agree, and give her a wink. ☺

So much FUN...

...and our day is not nearly done.

There's no time for me to tell it all; but one
thing is for sure, we're having a ball...

I love this holiday; it's a Bear-y special time —
laughter and love, and making Jesus shine!

Well y'all, I gotta go.

Come and say it with me —
"Ho-ho-ho!"

Have a "Bear-y Merry Christmas!"

Printed in the United States
By Bookmasters